Frogs

by

Gail Saunders-Smith

Pebble Books

an imprint of Capstone Press

1

7940273

Pebble Books

Pebble Books are published by Capstone Press
818 North Willow Street, Mankato, Minnesota 56001
http://www.capstone-press.com
Copyright © 1998 by Capstone Press
All Rights Reserved • Printed in the United States of America

Library of Congress Cataloging-in-Publication Data
Saunders-Smith, Gail.
  Frogs/by Gail Saunders-Smith.
  p.cm.
  Includes bibliographical references (p. 23) and index.
  Summary: Describes and illustrates the life cycle of frogs.
  ISBN 1-56065-484-8
  1. Frogs--Life cycles--Juvenile literature. [1. Frogs.] I. Title.

QL668.E2S18 1997
597.8'9--dc21
                      97-8308
                       CIP
                       AC

Editorial Credits
Lois Wallentine, editor; Timothy Halldin and James Franklin,
design; Michelle L. Norstad, photo research

Photo Credits
Dwight Kuhn, 14
Valan Photos/J.A. Wilkinson, cover; Jim Merli, 3 (right), 20;
  John Mitchell, 3 (left), 4, 6, 8, 10, 12; John Cancalosi, 1, 18;
  Herman H. Giethoorn, 16

2

Table of Contents

3

4

Frogs lay eggs.

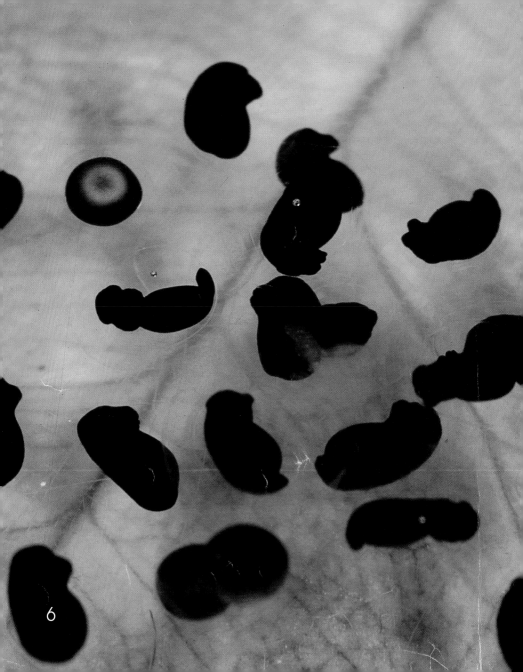

6

Eggs become
tadpoles.

8

Tadpoles have
tails.

Tadpoles grow
back legs.

Tadpoles grow
front legs.

The tails get shorter

and shorter

and shorter.

Tadpoles become frogs.

Words to Know

egg—the beginning stage of a frog

frog—a small green or brown animal that lives in the water and on land; a frog has webbed feet for swimming and long back legs for jumping

lay—to produce an egg or eggs

tadpole—the stage of a frog's growth between the egg and adult frog stages; tadpoles live in water

Read More

Lacey, Elizabeth. *The Complete Frog: A Guide for the Very Young Naturalist.* New York: Lothrop, Lee, and Shepard Books, 1989.

Pascoe, Elaine. *Tadpoles.* Woodbridge, Conn.: Blackbirch Press, Inc., 1997.

Pfeffer, Wendy. *From Tadpole to Frog.* New York: Harper Collins, 1994.

Internet Sites

The Froggy Page
http://frog.simplenet.com/froggy

Frog Life Cycle
http://www.geocities.com/TheTropics/1337/info.html

The Somewhat Amusing World of Frogs
http://www.csu.edu.au/faculty/commerce/account/frogs/frog.htm

Note to Parents and Teachers

This book describes and illustrates the life cycle of a frog. The clear photographs support the beginning reader in making and maintaining the meaning of the text. The plural nouns and simple verbs match the photograph on each page. The limited repetition supports the beginning reader while offering new vocabulary. Children may need assistance in using the Table of Contents, Words to Know, Read More, Internet Sites, and Index/Word List sections of the book.

Index/Word List

Word Count: 28